CRITICISM

CRITICISM

*An Essay on
Function, Form and Method*

BY

W. C. BROWNELL

KENNIKAT PRESS, INC./PORT WASHINGTON, N.Y.

82378

CRITICISM

TO BRANDER MATTHEWS

CRITICISM

I

FIELD AND FUNCTION

CRITICISM itself is much criticized,—which logically establishes its title. No form of mental activity is commoner, and, where the practice of anything is all but universal, protest against it is as idle as apology for it should be superfluous. The essentially critical character of formularies alleging the inferiority to books of the books about books that Lamb preferred, finding the genesis of criticism in creative failure, and so on, should of itself demonstrate that whatever objection may be made to it in practice there can be none in theory. In which case the only sensible view is that its practice should be perfected rather than abandoned. However, it is probably only in — may one say? — 'uncritical circles,' notoriously as skeptical about logic as about criticism, that it encounters this fundamental censure. 'Nobody here,' Lord Morley remarked, addressing the English Association, 'will undervalue criticism or fall into the gross blunder of regarding it as a mere parasite of creative work.' And, indeed, it would be slighting just proportion and intellectual decorum to lay any particular stress on the aspersions of the sprightly sciolists of the studios, such as, for example, the late Mr. Whistler, and of brilliant literary adventurers, such as, for another instance, the late Lord Beaconsfield.

As a matter of fact these two rather celebrated disparagers of criticism were greatly indebted to the critical faculty,

very marked in each of them. It is
now becoming quite generally appreci-
ated, I imagine, — thanks to criticism,
— that Degas's admonition to Whistler about his conduct cheapening his
talent, which every one will remember, embodied a slight misconception.
Whistler's achievements in painting,
however incontestable their merits,
would certainly have enjoyed less of
the vogue he so greatly prized had his
prescription that work should be 'received in silence' been followed in his
own case by himself. And it was certainly the critical rather than the creative element in Disraeli's more serious
substance that gave it the interest it
had for his contemporaries, and has
now altogether lost.

More worth while recalling than
Disraeli's inconsistency, however, is the
fact that in plagiarizing he distorted
Coleridge's remark, substituting 'crit-

ics' for 'reviewers' as those who had failed in creative fields. The substitution is venial in so far as in the England of that day the critics were the reviewers. But this is what is especially noteworthy in considering the whole subject: namely, that in England, as with ourselves, the art of criticism is so largely the business of reviewing as to make the two, in popular estimation at least, interconvertible terms. They order the matter differently in France. Every one must have been struck at first by the comparative slightness of the reviewing in French journalism. One's impression at first is that they take the business much less seriously than one would expect in a country with such an active interest in art and letters. The papers, even the reviews, concern themselves with the current product chiefly in the 'notice' or the *compte rendu*, which aims merely to inform the reader as to the contents of the book or the contributions to the exposition, whatever it may be, with but a meagre addition of comment either courteous or curt. The current art criticism even of Gautier, even of Diderot for that matter, is largely descriptive. In the literary *revues* what we should call the reviewing is apt to be consigned to a few back pages of running *chronique*, or a supplementary leaflet.

Of course one explanation is that the French public reads and sees for itself too generally to need or savor extensive treatment of the essentially undifferentiated. The practice of reviewing scrupulously all the output of the novel factories, exemplified by such periodicals as even the admirable *Athenæum*, would seem singular to it. But with us, even when the literature reviewed is eminent and serious, it is estimated, when it is reviewed with competence, by the anonymous expert, who confines himself to the matter in hand and delivers a kind of bench decision in a circumscribed case. And in France this is left to subsequent books or more general articles, with the result of releasing the critic for more personal work of larger scope. Hence, there are a score of French critics of personal quality for one English or American. Even current criticism becomes a province of literature instead of being a department of routine. Our own current criticism, anonymous or other, is, I need not say, largely of this routine character, when it has character, varied by the specific expert decision in a very few quarters, and only occasionally by a magazine *article de fond* of a real synthetic value. This last I should myself like to see the Academy, whose function must be mainly critical, encourage by every means open to it, by way of giving more *standing* to our criticism, which is what I think it needs first of all.

For the antipathy to criticism I imagine springs largely from confounding it with the reviewing — which I do not desire to depreciate, but to distinguish from criticism of a more personal order and a more permanent appeal. The tradition of English reviewing is impressive, and it is natural that Coleridge should have spoken of reviewers as a class, and that Mr. Birrell should have them exclusively in mind in defining the traits of the ideal critic. And we ourselves are not without journals which review with obvious resources of scholarship and skill, and deliver judgments with the tone, if not always with the effect, of finality. But of course, taking the country as a whole, reviewing is the least serious concern of the journalism that seems to take so many things lightly. And it is this reviewing that I fancy the authors and artists have in mind when they disparage criticism. They disparage it in the main, however, as insufficiently expert, but though I dare say this is often just, the objection to it which is apparently not considered, but which I should think even more considerable, is its tendency to monopolize the critical field and establish this very ideal of specific expertness, which its practice so frequently fails to realize, as the ideal of criticism in general. This involves, I think, a restricted view of the true critic's field, and an erroneous view of his function. Virtually it confines his own field to that of the practice he criticizes; and his function to that of estimating any practice with reference to its technical standards. In a word, expert criticism is necessarily technical criticism, and, not illogically, those whose ideal it is insist that the practitioner himself is the only proper critic of his order of practice.

This was eminently the view of the late Russell Sturgis, who had an inexhaustible interest in technic of all kinds and maintained stoutly that only artists should write about art. And though his own practice negatived his principle so far as painting and sculpture are concerned, that was perhaps because the painters and sculptors were themselves so remiss in lending a hand to the work he deemed it important to have done. They were surely excusable, in many cases, since they could allege preoccupation with what they could do even better, in proportion as they were either satisfactorily good at it or successful with it. Sturgis's theory was that art should be interpreted from the artist's point of view, assuming of course the existence of such a point of view. As a matter of fact there is none, and when it is sought what is found is either *an* artist's point of view, which is personal and not professional, or else it is that of every one else sufficiently educated in the results which artists could hardly have produced for centuries without, sooner or later, at least betraying what it is their definite aim distinctly to express. The esoteric in their work is a matter, not of art, — the universal language in which they communicate, — but of science; it does not reside in the point of view, but in the process.

All artistic accomplishment divides itself naturally, easily, and satisfactorily, however loosely, into the two categories, moral and material. The two certainly overlap, and this is particularly true of the plastic arts, whose peculiarity — or whose distinction, if you choose — is to appeal to the senses as well as to the mind. A certain technic therefore — that is to say, the science of their material side — is always to be borne in mind. But a far less elaborate acquaintance with this than is vital to the practitioner is ample for the critic, who may in fact easily have too much of it if he have any inclination to exploit rather than to subordinate it. He may quite conceivably profit by Arnold's caution: 'To handle these matters properly, there is needed a poise so perfect that the least overweight in any direction tends to destroy the balance . . . even erudition may destroy it. Little as I know therefore, I am always apprehensive, in dealing with poetry, lest even that little should [quoting a remark by the Duke of Wellington] "prove too much for my abilities."'

CRITICISM

The artist who exacts more technical expertness from the critic than he finds is frequently looking in criticism for what it is the province of the studio to provide; he requires of it the educational character proper to the classroom, or the qualifications pertinent to the hanging committee. Now, even confined within its proper limits, this esoteric criticism suffers from its inherent concentration on technic. Artistic innovation meets nowhere with such illiberal hostility as it encounters in its own hierarchy, and less on temperamental than on technical grounds. On the other hand, a painter like Bouguereau may systematically invert the true relations of conception and execution, employing the most insipid conventionalities to express his exquisite drawing, and remain for a generation the head of the professional corner in a school edifice where the critical faculty seems sometimes paralyzed by the technical criterion. And of course in technical circles such a criterion tends to establish itself. Millet, who refused to write about a fellow painter's work for the precise reason that he was a painter himself and therefore partial to his own different way of handling the subject, was a practitioner of exceptional breadth of view, and would perhaps have agreed with Aristotle, who, as Montaigne says, 'will still have a hand in everything,' and who asserts that the proper judge of the tiller is not the carpenter but the helmsman. Indeed, 'The wearer knows where the shoe pinches' is as sound a maxim as '*Ne sutor ultra crepidam*'; and the authority of the latter itself may be invoked in favor of leaving criticism to critics. The classics of æsthetic criticism constitute an impressive body of literature, which has been of immense interpretative service to art, and to which the only practising contributor of signal importance, it is worth bearing in mind, was himself a littérateur — even a novelist and a poet. Nor does it seem singular that, as a rule and in proportion to his seriousness, the practitioner should be engrossed by practice.

It is true that we have in America — possibly in virtue of our inevitable eclecticism — a considerable number of practising artists who also write distinguished criticism. But to ascribe its excellence to their technical expertness, rather than to their critical faculty and literary ability, would really be doing an injustice to the felicity with which they subordinate in their criticism all technical parade beyond that which is certainly too elementary to be considered esoteric. Certainly some of them would be indisposed to measure work by their own practice, and in that case what critical title does this practice in itself confer? As a rule indeed, I think, they rather help than hinder the contention that criticism is a special province of literature with, in fact, a technic of its own in which they show real expertness, instead of a literary adjunct of the special art with which it is variously called upon to concern itself. And in this special province, material data are far less considerable than moral — with which latter, accordingly, it is the special function of criticism to deal. Every one is familiar with plastic works of a perfection that all the technical talk in the world would not explain, as no amount of technical expertness could compass it. However young the artist might have begun to draw, or model, or design, whatever masters he might have had, however long he might have practised his art, whatever his skill, native or acquired, whatever his professional expertness, in a word, no artist could have achieved the particular result in question without those *qualities* which have controlled the result, and which it is the function of criticism to signalize, as it is the weakness of expert evaluation to neglect.

Criticism, thus, may not inexactly be described as the statement of the concrete in terms of the abstract. It is its function to discern and characterize the abstract qualities informing the concrete expression of the artist. Every important piece of literature, as every important work of plastic art, is the expression of a personality, and it is not the material of it, but the mind behind it, that invites critical interpretation. Materially speaking, it is its own interpretation. The concrete absorbs the constructive artist whose endeavor is to give substance to his idea, which until expressed is an abstraction. The concern of criticism is to measure his success by the correspondence of his expression to the idea it suggests and by the value of the idea itself. The critic's own language, therefore, into which he is to translate the concrete work he is considering, is the language of the abstract; and as in translation what is needed is appreciation of the foreign tongue and expertness in one's own, it is this language that it behooves him especially to cultivate.

As it is the *qualities* of the writer, painter, sculptor, and not the *properties* of their productions, that are his central concern, as his function is to disengage the moral value from its material expression, — I do not mean of course in merely major matters, but in minutiæ as well, such as even the lilt of a verse or the drawing of a wrist, the distinction being one of kind, not of rank, — qualities, not properties, are the very substance and not merely the subject of the critic's own expression. The true objects of his contemplation are the multifarious elements of truth, beauty, goodness, and their approximations and antipodes, underlying the various phenomena which express them, rather than the laws and rules peculiar to each form of phenomenal expression; which, beyond acquiring the familiarity needful for adequate appreciation, he may leave to the professional didacticism of each. And in thus confining itself to the art and eschewing the science of whatever forms its subject — mindful mainly of no science, indeed, except its own — criticism is enabled to extend its field while restricting its function, and to form a distinct province of literature, while relinquishing encroachments upon the territory of more exclusively constructive art.

FIELD AND FUNCTION

Of course thus individualizing the field and the function of criticism neither predicates universal capacity in nor prescribes universal practice to the individual critic, who however will specialize all the more usefully for realizing that both his field and his function are themselves as special as his faculty is universally acknowledged to be.

II

EQUIPMENT

THE critic's equipment consequently should be at least commensurate with the field implied by this view of his function. But it should really even exceed it, on the well-known principle that no one knows his subject who knows his subject alone. And this implies for criticism the possession of that cognate culture without which specific erudition produces a rather lean result. If, which is doubtful, it achieves rectitude, it misses richness. The mere function of examining and estimation can hardly be correctly conducted without illumination from the sidelights of culture. But certainly if criticism is to have itself any opulence and amplitude, any body and energy, it must bring to its specific business a supplementary fund of its own. If literature — or art as well for that matter — is a criticism of life, criticism in a similar sense and in the same degree determines the relations of the two, and thus needs as close touch with life as with art and letters. Thus, whatever the subject, the critical equipment calls for a knowledge of life, and in proportion to its depth and fullness, a philosophy of life. In no other way, indeed, can the critic's individuality achieve outline, and the body of his work attain coherence.

Obviously, therefore, that general culture which is a prerequisite to any philosophy of life is a necessity of his equipment, without which he can neither estimate his subject aright nor significantly enrich his treatment to the end of producing what constitutes literature in its turn — an ideal which, as

CRITICISM

I have already intimated, exhibits the insufficiency of what is known as expert criticism. And of this general culture, I should call the chief constituents history, æsthetics, and philosophy. 'The most profitable thing in the world for the institution of human life is history,' says Froissart; and the importance of history to any criticism which envisages life as well as art and letters, would need no more than mention were it not in fact so frequently and so generally overlooked by those who unconsciously or explicitly take the belletristic or purely æsthetic view of criticism. Since Taine such a view seems curiously antiquated. Evidently however it underlies much current practice, which appears to assume that current critical material is the product of spontaneous generation and that, accordingly, even its direct ancestry, as well as its ancestral influences, is negligible. And the same view is apparently held, not only in the class-room, but in what we may call professional circles, where both reasoning and research are so often strictly confined within the rigid limits of the special branch of study pursued or expounded.

Art and letters are nevertheless neither fortuitous phenomena, on the one hand, to be savored and tested merely by the sharp senses of the impressionist, nor, on the other, technical variants of an isolated evolution. Poetry for instance is neither pure music nor pure prosody. Even that of Blake or Whitman cannot be correctly judged by the senses unilluminated by the light that history sheds on its conformity to or deflection from the ideal laws to which legitimately it is responsible; *a fortiori*, of course, in the case of poetry that is truly expressive instead of melodiously or otherwise explosive. But in general the criticism that either correctly estimates or successfully contributes to art or letters rests firmly on that large and luminous view of life and the world which alone furnishes an adequately flexible standard for measuring whatever relates to life and the world, and which is itself furnished by history alone. Of course no one would prescribe a minute knowledge of the Carthaginian constitution any more than of the reasons for the disappearance of the digamma as a necessity of critical equipment, but a lack of interest in the distinctly cultural chapters of the book of human life witnesses, one would think, a lack of even that spirit of curiosity characteristic of the dilettante himself and naturally leading him beyond the strict confines of belles-lettres and pure æsthetics.

Æsthetics, however, in their broader aspect may be commended to even the purely literary critic as an important element of his ideal equipment at the present day. They constitute an element of cognate culture which imposes itself more and more, and literary critics who deem them negligible are no doubt becoming fewer and fewer. No one could maintain their parity with history as such an element, I think, for the reason that they deal with a more restricted field. On the other hand, the extent rather than the particularity of this field is now increasingly perceived, and the prodigious part played by the plastic in the history of human expression is receiving a recognition long overdue. I remember once, many years ago, a number of us were wasting time in playing one of those games dear to the desultory, consisting in making lists of the world's greatest men. We had discussed and accredited perhaps a dozen, when Homer

Martin, being asked to contribute, exclaimed, 'Well, I think it's about time to put in an artist or two.' The list was revised, but less radically, I imagine, than it would be to-day.

In France to-day no literary critic with a tithe of Sainte-Beuve's authority would be likely to incur the genuine compassion expressed for Sainte-Beuve when he ventured to talk about art by the Goncourts in their candid Diary. In England such a critic as Pater owes his reputation quite as much probably to his sense for the plastic as to his Platonism. In Germany doubtless the importance of æsthetics as a constituent of general culture has been generally felt since Lessing's time, and could hardly fail of universal recognition in the shadow of Goethe. With us in America, progress in this very vital respect has notoriously been slower, and it is not uncommon to find literary critics who evince, or who even profess, an ignorance of art that is more or less consciously considered by them a mark of more concentrated literary seriousness. And if an Academy of Arts *and* Letters should contribute in the least to remove this misconception it would disclose one *raison-d'être* and justify its modest pretensions. For so far as criticism is concerned with the æsthetic element, the element of beauty, in literature, a knowledge of æsthetic history and philosophy, theory and practice, serves it with almost self-evident pertinence.

The principles of art and letters being largely identical, æsthetic knowledge in the discussion of belles-lettres answers very much the purpose of a diagram in a demonstration. In virtue of it the critic may transpose his theme into a plastic key, as it were, and thus get nearer to its essential artistic quality by looking beyond the limitations of its proper technic. Similarly useful the art critic of any distinction has always found literary culture, and if this has led him sometimes to overdo the matter, it has been due not to his knowledge of literature but to his ignorance of art. But this ignorance is measurably as incapacitating to the critic of belles-lettres, whose ability to deal with the plastic that can only be felt must manifestly be immensely aided by an education in the plastic that can be seen as well. And for the critic of thought as well as of expression, the critic who deals with the relations of letters to life, the culture that is artistic as well as literary has the value inherent in acquaintance with the history and practice of one of the most influential, inspiring, and illuminating fields that the human spirit has cultivated almost from the beginning of time.

EQUIPMENT

Finally, since nothing in the way of cognate knowledge comes amiss in the culture pertinent to criticism, to the history and æsthetics of the critic's equipment, a tincture at least of philosophic training may be timidly prescribed. I am quite aware that this must be sparingly cultivated. Its peculiar peril is pedantry. Drenched in philosophy, the critical faculty is almost certain to drown. This faculty, when genuine, however, is so constituted that a smattering of philosophy makes a saturated solution for it. And such training in the realm of abstract thought, as *some* practice with its terms and processes involves, will help the critic in his thinking — which is, after all, his main business. It will serve to coördinate his analysis, and it will purge his constructive expression of incongruities, even if it endue this with no greater cogency and supply it with no additional energy. For criticism, dealing, as I have said, with the abstract, — though with the abstract held as closely to the concrete as a translation to the original, — the grammar of the abstract is as useful as its rhetoric is in general superfluous. What it needs is the ability to 'play freely' with such elements of the abstract as it can use, avoiding sedulously the while contagion from the petrifaction of its systems in which the concrete, which is the constant preoccupation of criticism, disappears from view. Duly on his guard against its insidious attractions, the critic may surely justify himself in his endeavor to make the abstract serve him by such examples as Aristotle, Longinus, Goethe, and Coleridge, not to mention Arnold, who with less training in it would have attacked it with far less success. It is at all events, in whatever degree it may prove adequate or become excessive, thoroughly pertinent to a matter so explicitly involving the discussion of principles as well as of data.

Examples in abundance fortify the inherent reasonableness of this general claim for what I have called cognate culture. The 'cases' confirm the theory, which of course otherwise they would confute. The three great modern critics of France show each in his own way the value of culture in the critical equipment. Sainte-Beuve's criticism is what it is largely because of his saturation with literature in general, not belles-lettres exclusively; of the sensitiveness and severity of taste thus acquired, or at least thus certified and invigorated; and of the instinctive ease, and almost scientific precision, with which he was thus enabled to apply in his own art that comparative method already established in the scientific study of linguistics and literary history. Thus, too, he was enabled to add perhaps his most distinguished contribution to the practice of criticism — the study, sympathetic but objective, of character, namely, the personality of the author which informs and explains his productions, and in which his productions inevitably inhere so far as they have any synthetic value, or significant purpose. Such study can only be pursued in the light of standards furnished by the sifting of innumerable examples, and illustrated in the work of the surviving fittest. Moreover the range within which Sainte-Beuve's exquisite critical faculty operated so felicitously acquired an extension of dignity and authoritativeness, quite beyond the reach of belles-lettres, in the production of his massive and monumental history of Port Royal. His culture, in a word, as well as his native bent, was such as considerably to obscure the significance of his having 'failed' in early experimentation as a novelist and as a poet!

How predominant the strain of scholarship and philosophic training is in the criticism of Taine it is superfluous to point out; the belletristic fanatics have been so tireless in its disparagement that at the present time, probably, his chief quality is popularly esteemed his characteristic defect. It is true that, though serving him splendidly, his philosophy on occasion dominates him rather despotically. After all, the critical faculty should preside in the critic's reflection, and not abdicate in favor of system — should keep on weighing and judging, however directed by philosophy and erudition, and not lapse into advocacy or administration. Poise, one of the chief critical requirements, settles into immobility in Taine. His point of view is so systematically applied that his criticism certainly, as I think his history also, is colored by it. But the colors are brilliant in any case, and if now and then untrue, are sure of correction by contemporary lenses, which are rather discreditably adjusted to depreciate his superb achievements — at least among English readers for whom he has done so much. And the apt consideration for our present purpose is the notable *service* which his philosophy and history have rendered a remarkable body of criticism, both æsthetic and literary; not the occasional way in which they invalidate its conclusiveness. Almost all histories of English literature are inconsecutive and desultory, or else congested and casual, compared with Taine's great work — whose misappreciations, as I say, correct themselves for us, but whose stimulus remains exhaustless.

And one may say that he has established the criticism of art on its present basis. The *Lectures* and the *Travels in Italy* first vitally connected art with life, and demonstrated its true title by recognizing it as an expression rather than an exercise. Certainly the latter phase demands interpretative treatment also, and it would be idle to ignore in Taine a lack of the sensuous sensitiveness that gives to Fromentin's slender volume so much more than a purely technical interest; just as it would be to look in him for the exquisite appreciation of personal idiosyncrasy possessed by Sainte-Beuve. But in his treatment of art as well as of literature, the philosophic structure around which he masses and distributes his detail is of a stability and significance of design that amply atones for the misapplication or misunderstanding of some of the detail itself.

Another instance of the value of culture in fields outside strictly literary and æsthetic confines, though, as I am contending, strictly cognate to them, is furnished by the Essays of Edmond Scherer. To the comparative personal and circumstantial judgments of Sainte-Beuve, to the systematic historical and evolutionary exposition of Taine, there succeeded in Scherer the point of view suggested rather than defined in the statement of Rod to the effect that Scherer judged not with his intelligence but with his character. Rod meant his epigram as a eulogy. Professor Saintsbury esteems it a betrayal, his own theory of criticism being of the art-for-art's-sake order, finding its justification in that 'it helps the ear to listen when the horns of Elf-land blow,' and denying to it, or to what he calls

36

'pure literature,' any but hedonistic sanctions — piquant philosophy, it has been observed, for a connoisseur without a palate.

Character at all events forms a signal element in the judgments of Scherer's austere and elevated criticism, and if it made him exacting in the presence of the frivolous, the irresponsible, and the insincere, and limited his responsiveness to the comic spirit, as it certainly did in the case of Molière, it undoubtedly made his reprehensions significant and his admirations authoritative. He began his career as a *pasteur*, and though he gradually reached an agnostic position in theology, he had had an experience in itself a guarantee, in a mind of his intelligence, of spirituality and high seriousness in dealing with literary subjects, and as absent from Sainte-Beuve's objectivity as from Taine's materialistic determinism. Without Renan's sinuous charm and truly catholic openmindedness, this Protestant-trained theologian turned critic brings to criticism not merely the sinews of spiritual centrality and personal independence, but a philosophic depth and expertness in reasoning that set him quite apart from his congeners, and establish for him a unique position in French literature. Criticism has never reached a higher plane in literature conceived as, in Carlyle's words, 'the Thought of Thinking Souls'; and it holds it not only in virtue of a native ideality and a perceptive penetration that atone in soundness for whatever they may lack in plasticity, but also, it is not to be doubted, in virtue of the severe and ratiocinative culture for which Geneva has stood for centuries.

III

CRITERION

ITS equipment established, criticism calls for a criterion. Sainte-Beuve says somewhere that our liking anything is not enough, that it is necessary to know further whether we are right in liking it — one of his many utterances that show how thoroughly and in what classic spirit he later rationalized his early romanticism.

The remark judges in advance the current critical impressionism. It involves more than the implication of Mr. Vedder's well-known retort to the time-honored philistine boast, 'I know nothing of art, but I know what I like': 'So do the beasts of the field.' Critical impressionism, intelligent and scholarly, such as that illustrated and advocated by M. Jules Lemaître and M. Anatole France, for example, though it may, I think, be strictly defined as appetite, has certainly nothing gross about it, but, contrariwise, everything that is refined. Its position is, in fact, that soundness of criticism varies directly with the fastidiousness of the critic, and that consequently this fastidiousness cannot be too highly cultivated, since it is the court of final jurisdiction. It is, however, a court that resembles rather a star chamber in having the peculiarity of giving no reasons for its decisions. It has, therefore, at the outset an obvious disadvantage in the impossibility of validating its decisions for the acceptance of others. So far as this acceptance is concerned, it can only say, 'If you are as well endowed with taste, native and acquired, as I am, the chances are that you will feel in the same way.'

But it is of the tolerant essence of impressionism to acknowledge that there is no certainty about the matter. And, in truth, the material to be judged is too multifarious for the criterion of taste. Matthew Arnold's measure of a successful translation: that is, the degree in which it produces the same effect as the original to a sense competent to appreciate the original, is an instance of a sensible appeal to taste: first, because the question is comparatively simple; and secondly, because in the circumstances there can be no other arbiter. But such instances are rare, and the very fact that so much matter for criticism still remains matter of controversy proves the proverb that tastes differ and the corollary that there is no use in disputing about them. It is quite probable that M. France would find M. Lemaître's plays and stories insipid, and quite certain that M.

Lemaître would shrink from the strain of salacity in M. France's romance. High differentiation and the acme of aristocratic fastidiousness, which both of these critics illustrate, manifestly do not serve to unify their taste. There *is* no universal taste. And criticism to be convincing must appeal to some accepted standard. And the aim of criticism is conviction. Otherwise actuated it must be pursued on the art-for-art theory, which, in its case at least, would involve a loss of identity. Recording the adventures of one's soul among masterpieces, which is M. France's variant of Eugène Véron's definition of landscape, — the first formal appearance of the idea, I think, — 'painting one's emotions in the presence of nature,' must be a purely self-regardant exercise unless the reader has an answering soul and can himself authenticate the masterpieces.

Feeling the unsatisfactoriness of the impressionist's irresponsibility, the late Ferdinand Brunetière undertook a campaign in opposition to it. He began it, if I remember aright, in his lectures in this country nearly twenty years ago. These lectures, however, and the course of polemic which followed them excelled particularly, I think, in attack. They contained some very effective destructive criticism of mere personal preference, no matter whose, as a final critical criterion. Constructively, on the other hand, Brunetière was less conclusive. In a positive way he had nothing to offer but a defense of academic standards. He harked back to the classic canon — that canon in accordance with which were produced those works designed, as Stendhal says, 'to give the utmost possible pleasure to our great-grandfathers.'

The case might perhaps have been

better stated. Brunetière was devoted to the noble French literature of the seventeenth century. The august had no doubt a special attraction for the self-made scholar. Out of reach the aristocratic always looks its best — the less attainable the more admirable. But though he became a distinguished scholar, Brunetière retained the temperament of the schoolmaster, which was either native to him or the result of belated acquaintance, however thorough, with what French impatience calls the *déjà-vu*. It was because he had so explicitly learned that he wished always to teach.

Now there is nothing strictly to teach save the consecrated and the canonical, whereas criticism is a live art, and contemporaneousness is of its essence. Once codified, it releases the genuine critic to conceive new combinations, — the 'new duties' taught by 'new occasions,' — and becomes itself either elementary or obsolete. It is important to know which, of course, as Wordsworth's failure successfully to recast the catalogue of the poetic *genres*, noted by Arnold, piquantly attests. Moreover in his devotion to the seventeenth, Brunetière was blind to the eighteenth century, — as well as, by the way, heedless of Voltaire's warning that the only bad style is the *style ennuyeux;* his style alone devitalized his polemic in favor of prescription. Finally, instead of winning adherents for him, this ardent advocacy of authority took despotic possession of his entire mind and gathered him to the bosom of religious and political reaction.

Whatever our view of criticism, it is impossible at the present day to conceive it as formula, and the rigidity of rules of taste is less acceptable than the license permitted under the reign of taste unregulated, however irregular, individual, and irresponsible. In spite of the logical weakness of the impressionist theory, it is to be observed that a high level of taste, uniform enough to constitute a very serviceable arbiter, at least in circumstances at all elementary, is practically attainable; and as a matter of fact is, in France at least, often attained. For in criticism as elsewhere it is true that we rest finally upon instinct, and faith underlies reason. The impressionist may properly remind us that all proof, even Euclidian, proceeds upon postulates.

The postulates of criticism, however, are apt unsatisfactorily to differ from those of mathematics in being propositions taken for granted rather than self-evident. The distinction is radical. It is not the fact that everybody is agreed about them that gives axioms their validity, but their self-evidence.

Postulates that depend on the sanction of universal agreement, on the other hand, are conventions. Universal agreement may be brought about in a dozen ways. It may be imposed by authority, as in the case of classic criticism, or it may develop insensibly, illogically, and indefensibly; it may derive, not from truth but from tradition, or it may certainly be the result of general reaction, and promptly crystallize with a rigidity equivalent to that from which it is just emancipated. Examples would be superfluous. The conventions of romanticism, realism, impressionism, symbolism, or what-not, are no more intrinsically valid than those underlying the criticism of academic prescription, as is attested by this variability of the universal agreement which is their sanction.

The true postulates of criticism have hardly varied since Aristotle's day, and impressionism itself, in imagining its own an advance upon them, would be in peril of fatuity. Yet even sound intuitions, fundamental as they may be, do not take us very far. Pascal, who though one of the greatest of reasoners is always girding at reason, was obliged to admit that it does the overwhelming bulk of the work. 'Would to God,' he exclaims, 'that we had never any need of it, and knew everything by instinct and sentiment! But nature has refused us this blessing; she has, on the contrary, given us but very little knowledge of this kind, and all other knowledge can only be acquired by reasoning.' But even if intuitions had all the importance claimed for them, it would still be true that *conventions* are extremely likely to be disintegrated by the mere lapse of time into what every one sees to have been really inductions from practice become temporarily and more or less fortuitously general, and not genuine intuitive postulates at all. Still clearer is the conventionality of the systems erected upon them, beneath which as a matter of fact they customarily lie buried. All sorts of eccentricity are incident to elaboration, of course, whether its basis be sound or unsound.

So that, in brief, when the impressionist alleges that a correct judgment of a work of literature or art depends ultimately upon feeling, we are quite justified in requiring him to tell us *why* he feels as he does about it. It is not enough for him to say that he is a person of particularly sensitive and sound organization, and that his feeling, therefore, has a corresponding finality. In the first place, as I have said, it is impossible to find in the judgments derived from pure taste anything like the uniformity to be found in the equipment as regards taste of the judges themselves. But for all their fastidiousness these judges are as amenable as grosser spirits to the test of reason. And it is only rational that the first question asked of them when they appeal to the arbitrament of feeling should be: Is your feeling the result of direct intuitive perception, or of unconscious subscription to convention? Your true distinction from the beasts of the field surely should lie, not so much in your superior organization resulting in superior taste, as in freedom from the conventional, to which even in their appetites the beasts of the field, often extremely fastidious in this respect, are nevertheless notoriously enslaved. In a word, even if impressionism be philosophically sound in the impeachment of reason unsupported by intuitive taste, it cannot dethrone reason as an arbiter in favor of the taste that is not intuitive but conventional. The true criterion of criticism therefore is only to be found in the rationalizing of taste.

This position once reached, it is clear that the only way in which the impressionist, however cultivated, can be at all sure of the validity of the *feeling* on which he bases his judgment is by the exercise of his reasoning faculty. Only in this way can he hope to determine whether his 'impression' originates in a genuine personal perception of the relations of the object producing it to some self-evident principle of truth or beauty, or proceeds from habit, from suggestion, from the insensible pressure of current, which is even more potent than classic, convention. Absolutely certain of achieving this result, the critic can hardly expect to be. Nothing is more insidious than the conventional. Civilized life is continually

51

82378

paying it tribute in innumerable ways. Culture itself, so far as it is uncritical, is perhaps peculiarly susceptible to it. But the critic can discharge his critical duty only by approximating this certainty as nearly as possible, by processes of scrutiny, comparison, and reflection, and in general that arduous but necessary and not unrewarding exercise of the mind involved in the checking of sensation by thought.

There is nothing truistic at the present time in celebrating the thinking power, counselling its cultivation and advocating its application — at least within the confines of criticism where the sensorium has decidedly supplanted it in consideration. Nor, on the other hand, is there anything recondite in so doing. It is as plain as it used to be remembered that it is in 'reason' that a man is 'noble,' in 'faculty' that he is 'infinite,' in 'apprehension' that he is 'like a god.' The importance of his exquisite sensitiveness to impressions is a *post*-Shakespearean discovery. I certainly do not mean to belittle the value of this sensitiveness, in suggesting for criticism the advantages of its control by the thinking power, and in noting the practical disappearance of the latter from the catalogue of contemporary prescription. If my topic were not criticism, but performance in the field of American imaginative activity, to belittle taste would at the present time be unpardonable. The need of it is too apparent. The lack of it often cheapens our frequent expertness, ruptures the relation between truth and beauty, and is responsible for a monotonous miscellaneity that is relieved less often than we could wish by works of enduring interest.

It cannot, however, be maintained that the standard of pure taste is a wholly adequate corrective for this condition even in the field of performance. At least it has been tried, and the results have not been completely satisfactory. We have in literature more taste than we had in days when, perhaps, we had more talent. (I exclude the domain of scholarship and its dependencies, in which we have made, I should suppose, a notable advance.) But the very presence of taste has demonstrated its insufficiency. In general literature, indeed, if its presence has been marked, its effect is not very traceable, because it has been mainly exhibited in technic. It can't be said, I think, to have greatly affected the substance of our literary production. In two of the arts, however, taste has long had full swing with us — the arts, I mean, of architecture and sculpture; and the appreciation it has met with in these is, though general, not rarely of

the kind that confuses the merits of the
decorative with those of the monumental, and the virtues of adaptation with
those of design. A rational instead of a
purely susceptible spirit, dictating constructive rather than merely appreci-
ative and assimilative activity, might
have been more richly rewarded in these
fields — might even have resulted in
superior taste.

In the restricted field of criticism, at
all events, the irresponsibility of pure
temperament seems currently so popular as to imply a general belief that
reasoning in criticism died with Macaulay and is as defunct as Johnson, having given place to a personal disposition
which perhaps discounts its prejudices
but certainly caresses its predilections
as warrant of 'insight' and 'sympathy.'
Yet our few star examples in current
criticism are eminently critics who give
reasons for the hope that is in them; and

certainly American literature has one
critic who so definitely illustrated the
value of the thinking power in criticism
that he may be said almost to personify
the principle of critical ratiocination. I
mean Poe. Poe's perversities, his cav-
illing temper, his unscrupulousness in
praise if not in blame, his personal irresponsibility, invalidate a great deal of
his criticism, to say nothing of its dog-
matic and mechanical character. But
at its best it is the expression of his altogether exceptional reasoning faculty.
His reasons were not the result of reflection, and his ideas were often the
crotchets Stedman called them; but he
was eminently prolific in both, and his
handling of them was expertness itself.
His ratiocination here has the artistic
interest it had in those of his tales that
are based on it, and that are imaginative
as mathematics is imaginative. And his
dogmas were no more conventions than

his conclusions were impressions. His criticism was equally removed from the canonical and the latitudinarian. If he stated a proposition he essayed to demonstrate it, and if he expressed a preference he told *why* he had it.

Poe's practice is, indeed, rather baldly ratiocinative than simply rational, and its felicity in his case does not, it is true, disguise its somewhat stark, exclusive, and exaggerated effect. I do not cite M. Dupin as an example of the perfect critic. There is something debased — not to put too fine a point upon it — in the detective method wherever used. It is not merely subtle, but serpentine — too tortuous and too terrene for the ampler upper air of examination, analysis, and constructive comment. Reason is justified of her children, not of her caricaturists. But if the answer to the question Why? which I have noted as her essential monopoly (since prescription precludes and impressionism scouts the inquiry), be challenged as an advantage to criticism, I think its value can be demonstrated in some detail.

The epicurean test of the impressionist, let me repeat, is of course not a standard, since what gives pleasure to some gives none to others. And some standard is a necessary postulate, not only of all criticism, but of all discussion or even discourse. Without one, art must indeed be 'received in silence,' as recommended by the persistently communicative Whistler. In literature and art there are, it is true, no longer any statutes, but the common law of principles is as applicable as ever, and it behooves criticism to interpret the cases that come before it in the light of these. Its function is judicial, and its business to weigh and reason rather than merely to testify and record. And if it belongs in the field of reason rather than in that of emotion, it must consider less the pleasure that a work of art produces than the worth of the work itself. This is a commonplace in ethics, where conduct is not approved by its happy result but by its spiritual worthiness. And if art and literature were felt to be as important as ethics, the same distinction would doubtless have become as universal in literary and art criticism. Which is of course only another way of stating Sainte-Beuve's contention that we need to know whether we are right or not when we are pleased. And the only guide to that knowledge — beyond the culture which, however immensely it may aid us, does not automatically produce conformity or secure conviction — is the criterion of reason applied to the work of ascertaining value apart from mere attractiveness. The attractiveness takes care of itself, as happiness does when we have done our duty.

At all events, aside from its superior philosophic satisfactoriness, thus indicated, a rational — rather than either an academic and authoritative or an impressionist and individual — criticism is especially useful, I think, at the present time, in two important particulars. It is, in the first place, especially fitted to deal with the current phase of art and letters. Of this phase, I take it, freedom and eclecticism are the main traits. Even followers of tradition exercise the freest of choices, tradition itself having become too multifarious to be followed *en bloc*. On the other hand, those who flout tradition and pursue the experimental, illustrate naturally still greater diversity. Both must ultimately appeal to the criterion of reason, for neither can otherwise justify its practice and pretensions. Prescription is a practical ideal if it is coherent; it loses its constituting sanction the moment it offers a choice. And experiment attains success only when through proof it reaches demonstration. In either case a criterion is ultimately addressed which is untrammeled by precedent and unmoved by change; which is strict without rigidity, and seeks the law of any performance within and not outside it; which demands no correspondence to any other concrete, but only to the appropriate abstract; which, in fact, substitutes for a concrete ideal a purely abstract one of intrinsic applicability to the matter in hand. It exacts titles, but they may be couched in any form, or expressed in any tongue but that of irrationality. No more the slave of schools than the sponsor of whim, it does not legislate, but judges performance, in its twofold aspect of conception and execution, in accordance with principles universally un-contested.

In the next place, no other criterion is competent to deal critically with the great question of our day in art and letters alike, namely, the relation of reality to the ideal. No other, I think, can hope to preserve disentangled the skein of polemic and fanaticism in which this question tends constantly to wind itself up into apparently inextri-cable confusion. Taste, surely, cannot. Taste, quite comprehensibly, I think, breathes a sigh of weariness whenever the subject of 'realism' is mentioned. Nevertheless, 'realism' is established, entrenched, and I should say impreg-nable to the assaults of its more radical and numerous foes, more particularly those of the art-for-art's-sake army. It is too fundamentally consonant with the current phase of the Time-Spirit to be in any present danger. But it is only reason that can reconcile its claims with those of its censors by showing wherein, and to what extent, 'realism' is really a catholic treatment of reality, and not a protestant and polemic gospel of the literal.

Reality has become recognized as the one vital element of significant art, and it seems unlikely that the unreal will ever regain the empire it once possessed. Its loss, at all events, is not ours, since it leaves us the universe. But it is obvious that 'realism' is often in practice, and not infrequently in conception, a very imperfect treatment of reality, which indeed not rarely receives more sympathetic attention in the romantic or even the classic household. Balzac is a realist, and at times the most artificial of great romancers. George Sand is a romanticist, and a very deep and fundamental reality not rarely underlies her superficial extravagances. Fundamentally, truth — which is certainly none other than reality — was her inspiration, as, fundamentally, it certainly was not always Balzac's. 'Realism' has made reality our touchstone. But it is not a talisman acting automatically if misapplied. To mistake the badge for the credentials of a doctrine is so frequent an error because it is irrational, and close-thinking, being difficult, is exceptional. Exponents of 'realism,' such as that most admirable of artists, Maupassant, are extraordinarily apt in practice to restrict the field of reality till the false proportion results in a quintessentially unreal effect. Every detail is real, but the implication of the whole is fantastic. Why? Because the ideal is excluded. The antithesis of reality is not the ideal, but the fantastic.

This is, I think, the most important distinction to bear in mind in considering the current realistic practice in all the arts. I refer of course to what we characterize as the ideal in general — not to the particular ideal whose interpenetration with the object constitutes the object a work of art and measures it as such. But for that matter the ideal in general may be conceived as having a similar relation to reality. Since it is a part of the order of the universe, — of reality, that is to say, — it is obviously not antithetic to it. On the other hand, the fantastic is essentially chaotic by definition though often speciously, attractively, and at times poetically garbed in the raiment of order — the poetry of Coleridge or the compositions of Blake, for example. The defect of this kind of art *is* its lack of reality, and its consequent comparative insignificance. But it is no more ideal for that reason than *Lear* or the Venus of Melos. This is still more apparent in the less artistic example of Hawthorne's tales, where in general the fantasticality consists in the garb rather than the idea, and where accordingly we can more readily perceive the unreality and consequent insignificance, the incongruous being more obvious in the material than in the moral field. But it is the special business of criticism at the present time of 'realistic' tyranny to avoid confusing the ideal with the fantastic, to avoid disparagement of it as opposed to reality, and to disengage it from elements that obscure without invalidating it.

Ivanhoe, for example, is fantastic history, but the character of the Templar is a splendid instance of the ideal inspiring, informing, intensifying, incontestable reality. In *Le Père Goriot*, on the other hand, in which the environment and atmosphere are realistic to the last degree, the protagonist is the mere personification of a passion. These are, no doubt, subtleties. But they are not verbal subtleties. They are inseparable from the business of criticism. And they impose on it the criterion of reason rather than that of feeling, which cannot be a standard, or that of precedent and prescription, which is outworn.

Finally, — and if I have hitherto elaborated to excess, here I need not elaborate at all, — no other than a rational criterion so well serves criticism in the most important of all its functions, that of establishing and determining the relation of art and letters to the life that is their substance and their subject as well.

METHOD

AND a rational criterion implies a constructive method. In itself analysis reaches no conclusion, which is the end and aim of reason. Invaluable as is its service in detail, some rational ideal must underlie its processes, and if these are to be fruitful they must determine the relations of the matter in hand to this ideal, and even in dissection contribute to the synthesis that constitutes the essence of every work of any individuality. The weak joint in Sainte-Beuve's armor is his occasional tendency to rest in his analysis. It is the finer art to suggest the conclusion rather than to draw it, no doubt, but one should at least do that; and I think Sainte-Beuve, in spite of his search for the *faculté maîtresse* and his anticipation of the race, the *milieu*, and the moment theory so hard worked by Taine, occasionally fails to justify his analysis in this way; so that his result is both artistically and philosophically inconclusive. Now and then he pays in this way for his aversion to pedantry and system, and the excessive disinterestedness of his curiosity.

It would certainly be pedantry to insist on truly constructive criticism in every *causerie du lundi* in which a great critic may quite pardonably vary his more important work with the play for which he has a *penchant*. But on the other hand truly constructive criticism does not of necessity involve rigidity. It implies not a system, but a method — to employ the distinction with which Taine defended his procedure, but which assuredly he more or less conspicuously failed to observe. It prescribes, in every work of criticism, a certain independence of its subject, and imposes on it the same constructive obligations that it in turn requires of its theme. A work of criticism is in fact as much a thesis as its theme, and the same thematic treatment is to be exacted of it. And considered in this way as a thesis, its unity is to be secured only by the development in detail of some central conception preliminarily established and constantly referred to, however arrived at, whether by intuition or analysis. The detail thus treated becomes truly contributive and constructive in a way open to no other method. We may say indeed that all criticism of moment, even impressionist criticism, has this synthetic aspect at least, as otherwise it must lack even the appearance of that organic quality necessary to effectiveness. And when we read some very interesting and dis-

tinguished criticism — such as the ag-
glutinate and amorphous essays of
Lowell, for example — and compare
it with concentric and constructive
work, — such as *par excellence* that of
Arnold, — we can readily see that its
failure in force is one of method as well
as of faculty.

On the other hand, the constructive
method is peculiarly liable to excess.
If the central conception it is concerned
with is followed out in detail without
the checks and rectifications of analysis — the great verifying process — we
have the partisanship of Carlyle, the
inelasticity of Taine, the prescriptive
formulary of Brunetière. The spirit of
system stifles freedom of perception and
distorts detail. Criticism becomes theoretic. And though theoretic criticism
may be, and in fact is not unlikely to be,
artistically effective, it is fatally un-
trustworthy, because it is bent on illus-

trating its theory in its analysis, instead of merely verifying such features of its central conception as analysis will confirm. Against such intuitive extravagance as Carlyle's the advantages of remarkable insight may fairly be set off. The academic prescriptions of Brunetière, too, have a distinct educational value — the results of a high-class literary scholiast are always technically instructive, however lacking they may be in the freedom and impressionability sanctioned by a criterion less rigid for being purely rational, and committed to no body of doctrine, traditional or other.

It is, however, the historical method of criticism that chiefly illustrates constructive excess. This method has at present probably the centre of the stage; and though there is in France a distinct reaction from the supremacy of Taine and in favor of Sainte-Beuve's sinuous plasticity, the method itself maintains its authority. Taine was an historian and a philosopher rather than a critic, and his criticism is accordingly not so much criticism illuminated by history and philosophy as philosophic history. The data of literature and art under his hand become the 'documents' of history, of which in a scientific age we hear so much. His thesis once established, however, as historical rather than literary or æsthetic, too much I think can hardly be said for his treatment. Classification has the advantage of clearing up confusion, and the value of a work like the *History of English Literature* appears when one recognizes its paramount merit as resident in the larger scope and general view of history in which of necessity purely individual traits are to some extent blurred if not distorted. These indeed may very well be left to pure criticism whose precise business they are. But the historic method in pure criticism is held quite independently of Taine's authority. Scherer, for example, arguing against 'personal sensations' in criticism, maintains that from the study of a writer's character and of his period the right understanding of his work issues spontaneously. This is excellent prescription for the impressionist, although Scherer doubtless means by 'personal sensations,' personal *judgment* also, and thus minimizes or indeed obliterates perhaps the most essential element of all in criticism, the critic's own personality. Scherer's practice, precisely owing to his personality, far excelled his theory, as to which Arnold reminded him of Macaulay, who certainly knew his writers and their period, but in whose mind a right understanding of their works occasionally failed spontaneously to issue.

METHOD

In fine, the historic method, great as have been its services to criticism and truly constructive as it is, has two erroneous tendencies. It tends generally to impose its historical theory on the literary and æsthetic facts, to discern their historical rather than their essential character; and, as inelastically applied, at all events, it tends specifically to accept its 'documents' as final rather than as the very *subjects* of its concern. Taine furnishes a striking instance of the latter practice. I have never myself been able to agree with those of his opponents, who, like Brunetière, rested in the comfortable assurance that his whole theory was overthrown by the fact that the ordinary Venetian gondolier of the period was the product of the influences that also produced Tintoretto. One might as well hold that immunity in some cases is not the result of the vaccine that fails to take in others; the causes of such differences in either physiology or history being perhaps, so far as they are not obvious, too obscure for profitable discussion compared with the causes of resemblances. But from the critical point of view it *is* a legitimate objection to his rigorous application of his method that he is led by it to consider so disproportionately *causes*, which are the proper subject of history, rather than *characteristics*, which are the true subject of criticism; to deem the business finished, so to say, when it is explained, and, comparatively speaking, to eschew its estimation.

As to the other tendency, that of imposing historical theory on critical data, it is a commonplace that history itself, which has been luminously called philosophy teaching by examples, sometimes suffers from the submergence of its examples by its philosophy. In criticism the result is more serious because, viewed in the same light, its 'examples' have a far more salient importance. They are themselves differentiated philosophically in a high degree, and it is correspondingly difficult successfully to treat them merely as pieces of some vaster mosaic. On large lines and in an elementary way, this may of course be usefully done, but the work belongs in general I think rather to the class-room than to the forum of criticism. In the latter place their traits call for a treatment at once more individually searching and more conformed to an abstract, ideal, independent, and rational standard — for the application to the data they furnish of the *ideas* they suggest, not the theory they fit.

Now, in the true critical field of independent judgment, however enlightened by culture and fortified by philosophic training, we know very well that theory means preconception. And, carried into any detail of prescription, preconception is as a matter of fact constantly being confuted by performance. Divorced from the ideas proper to each performance, reposing on a formula derived in its turn from previous performance become accepted and consecrate, it is continually disconcerted. New schools with new formulæ arise as if by some inherent law, precisely at the apogee of old ones. And preconception, based as it perforce is upon some former crystallization of the diverse and undulating elements of artistic expression, is logically inapplicable at any given time — *except* as it draws its authority from examples of permanent value and enduring appeal, in which case no one would think of calling it preconception at all. It may be said, to be sure, that philosophically this view, in excluding theory, degrades

criticism to an altogether ancillary sta-
tion — the business of merely furnish-
ing data for an historical synthesis.
But I am disinclined to accept this implication until the possibility of an historical synthesis at all comparable in
exactness with the critical determina-
tion of the data for it is realized or
shown to be realizable. The monu-
ment that Sainte-Beuve's critical essays constitute is, in spite of their dis-
proportionate analysis, far otherwise
considerable than the fascinating historical and evolutionary framework
within which Taine's brilliant synthesis
so hypnotizes our critical faculty.

In general effect, moreover, Sainte-
Beuve's work is itself markedly synthetic. What a complete picture it
presents, at the same time continually
illustrating the truth that the wiser
business of criticism is to occupy itself with examples and the ideas they

evoke, not with theories and the systems they threaten! For with examples we have the essential element of unity 'given'; it is actual, not problematical. And — impersonal theses of course aside — in criticism of the larger kind as distinct from mere reviewing or expert commentary, by examples we mean, practically, personalities. That is to say, not *Manfred*, but Byron, not the Choral Symphony, but Beethoven. I mean, naturally, so far as personality is expressed in work, and do not suggest invasion of the field of biography except to tact commensurable with that which so notably served Sainte-Beuve. There is here ample scope for the freest exercise of the synthetic method. For personality is the most concrete and consistent entity imaginable, mysteriously unifying the most varied and complicated attributes. The solution of this mystery is the end of critical research. To state it is the crown of critical achievement. The critic may well disembarrass himself of theoretical apparatus, augment and mobilize his stock of ideas, sharpen his faculties of penetration, and set in order all his constructive capacity, before attacking such a complex as any personality, worthy of attention at all, presents at the very outset. If he takes to pieces and puts together again the elements of its composition, and in the process or in the result conveys a correct judgment as well as portrait of the original thus interpreted, he has accomplished the essentially critical part of a task demanding the exercise of all his powers.

And I think he will achieve the most useful result in following the line I have endeavored to trace in the work of the true masters of this branch of literature, the born critics whose practice shows it to be a distinctive branch of literature, having a function, an equipment, a criterion, and a method of its own. This practice involves, let me recapitulate, the initial establishment of some central conception of the subject, gained from specific study illuminated by a general culture, followed by an analysis of detail confirming or modifying this, and concluding with a synthetic presentation of a physiognomy whose features are as distinct as the whole they compose — the whole process interpenetrated by an estimate of value based on the standard of reason, judging the subject freely after the laws of the latter's own projection, and not by its responsiveness to either individual whim or formulated prescription. This, at all events, is the ideal illustrated, with more or less closeness, by not only such critics as Sainte-Beuve, Scherer, and Arnold, but

METHOD

such straightforward apostles of pure
good sense as Sarcey and Émile Faguet.

How the critic conducts his criticism
will of course depend upon his own personality, and the ranks of criticism con-
tain perhaps as great a variety of types
and individuals as is to be found in any
other field of artistic expression.   For,
beyond denial, criticism is itself an art;
and, as many of its most successful
products have been entitled 'portraits,'
sustains a closer analogy at its best
with plastic portraiture than with such
pursuits as history and philosophy,
which seek system through science.
One of Sainte-Beuve's studies is as definitely a portrait as one of Holbein's;
and on the other hand a portrait by
Sargent, for example, is only more obviously and not more really, a critical
product than are the famous 'portraits'
that have interpreted to us the genera-
tions of the great.   More exclusively

imaginative art the critic must, it is true, forego. He would wisely, as I have contended, confine himself to portraiture and eschew the panorama. In essaying a 'School of Athens' he is apt, rather, to produce a 'Victory of Constantine.' His direct aim is truth even in dealing with beauty, forgetting which his criticism is menaced with transmutation into the kind of poetry that one 'drops into' rather than attains.

I have dwelt on the æsthetic as well as the literary field in the province of criticism, and insisted on the æsthetic element as well as the historic in the culture that criticism calls for, because in a very true and fundamental sense art and letters are one. They are so at all events in so far as the function of criticism is concerned, and dictate to this the same practice. Current philosophy may find a pragmatic sanction for a pluralistic universe, but in the criticism of art, whether plastic or literary, we are all 'monists.' The end of our effort is a true estimate of the data encountered in the search for that beauty which from Plato to Keats has been virtually identified with truth, and the highest service of criticism is to secure that the true and the beautiful, and not the ugly and the false, may in wider and wider circles of appreciation be esteemed to be the good.